the
ILLU

Lives of the *Saints*

Abridged Easy To Read Edition

Edited by

Victor Hoagland, C.P.

Regina
Press

Nihil Obstat: Reverend Robert O. Morrissey, J.C.D.

                   Censor librorum
                   June 16, 2003

Imprimatur: Most Reverend William Murphy
                   Bishop of Rockville Centre
                   June 23, 2003

THE REGINA PRESS
10 Hub Drive
Melville, New York 11747

Artwork © Copyright 2006 by The Bridgeman Art Library.
The Bridgeman Art Library International Ltd. is registered with Companies House in England as Limited Company 33324579 of 17-19 Garway Road London W2 4PH United Kingdom. Directors: Viscountess and Viscount Bridgeman.

Printed in China.

ISBN: 9780882710488

Dedication

Some people receive a special touch of God's grace. No two of them are alike. Some live into old age, others pass after only a few years on earth. Whatever their life span, their natural abilities or life's work, they are extraordinary human beings, who helped to change the world in which they lived.

Kathleen McBride was such a person. Though she was only on this earth for forty-one years, her life affected the lives of the many different people she came into contact with. Many believe that she was an angel sent by God to make people realize what is truly important in life – faith, family and friends. Her life served as an example to those who knew her. She believed that no obstacle in life was too great to overcome. In her last days, Kathleen informed those around her that she felt the purpose of her life was to glorify God. What a profound statement for her to make, knowing that she was soon going to be reunited with her Lord.

The world is a better place because Kathleen lived. All of those who knew her will never forget her. This book is dedicated to her memory. May she rest in peace.

Sandro Botticelli. *The Coronation of the Virgin*, (1444/5-1510)
Galleria degli Uffizi, Florence, Italy

Table of Contents

Foreword

Through the ages some people receive a special touch of God's grace. We call them saints. They come from many nations and races. No two of them are alike. Some live into old age; others pass only a few years on earth. Whatever their life span, their natural abilities or lifework, they are extraordinary human beings who ennoble our human family. The world is better because they have lived.

This book is about some of the most popular saints remembered in the calendar of the Catholic Church. Apostles, martyrs, bishops and missionaries, holy men and women who loved God and his people in a remarkable way. Some died for their faith in Christ; others served the poor, upheld the cause of justice, pursued truth and prayed to God with exceptional results. Like leaven in the earth's mass, they changed the world in which they lived.

The saints lifted the spirits of the men and women of their time who marveled at their likeness to Christ. We today recall them so that our spirits might be lifted up too. Their heroic lives inspire us, their love and fidelity challenges us, and their prayers support us. They are companions for our journey of faith.

Bartolome Esteban Murillo. *Madonna and Child,* (1618-1682)
Palazzo Pitti, Florence, Italy

JANUARY

MARY, THE MOTHER OF GOD — January 1

The Christian year begins with a feast in honor of Mary, the Mother of God. First among the saints, she is the loving mother of Jesus and mother of us all.

God chose Mary for a special role in history. She was to give birth to the Messiah, whom God would send to save all people from sin and bring joy and peace to the world. Like a new Eve, Mary became the "Mother of all the living" because her child could bring all generations new life. The prophets of the Old Testament spoke of her in their promise that a virgin would bear a son whose name is Emmanuel, "God with us." And St. Paul would describe her role in this way: "When the fullness of time came, God sent his Son born of woman…"

God prepared Mary with special care and grace. Coming to her home at Nazareth, the Angel Gabriel hailed her as "full of grace," the beloved of the Holy Spirit. Even before her birth, God made her holy and free from sin.

Mary's response to the angel reveals her own inner spirit. "Behold the handmaid of the Lord, be it done to me according to your word." Freely and wholeheartedly Mary gave herself to God and committed herself to her son, Jesus, his life and mission.

The intimate union of Jesus and Mary is described in the Gospels. At the angel's visit, Mary conceived her child and in joy hastened to visit her cousin, Elizabeth, whose own child, John, would prepare the Savior's way. With delight Mary showed her newborn son to the shepherds and the Magi as they came to Bethlehem in search of a savior. She presented Jesus in the temple and heard the old man Simeon foretell that a sword of sorrow and contradiction would strike them both. She sorrowed at the loss of Jesus on a pilgrimage to Jerusalem and treasured in her heart his words and the things he did.

When Jesus began his public life, Mary remained at his side. At the marriage feast of Cana, her words of sympathy for the newly married couple prompted his first miracle. She journeyed with him to Calvary and stood faithfully beneath his cross where, with love and acceptance, she joined in the sacrifice of her dying son. Finally, she accepted the mission Jesus himself would give her in his last moments. Turning to his disciple, John, who represented all of his disciples, Jesus said to her: "Woman, behold your son."

Mary offered a mother's love to the Church that waited for the coming of the Holy Spirit at

Pentecost. And when her days on earth were done, she was taken up to heaven to reign among the saints in glory.

Mary still shares in the mission of Jesus, her son. With motherly care she intercedes for those who journey now on earth facing trials and difficulties. She renews faith and love in all who turn their eyes to her.

From the earliest days of the Church till the present, Mary has been honored for the gifts God has given her and the favors she has bestowed on the world. "All generations shall call me blessed, for he who is mighty has done great things to me," she prophesied in her Magnificat. The many feasts of Mary during the year are a sign of her close association in the mysteries of Jesus, as well as the Christian people's love for her over the centuries.

In the days of Advent and the Christmas season, she is frequently recalled for her special role in the birth of Jesus. The Solemnity of Mary, the Mother of God (January 1), celebrates her place in God's plan of redemption. Two other "Christmas" feasts during the year also honor her: the Annunciation of the Angel Gabriel (March 25) and the Presentation of Jesus in the Temple (February 2).

The Solemnity of the Immaculate Conception (December 8) celebrates the belief that Mary from her conception in the womb of her mother, Ann, was preserved from all stain of original sin. The

Solemnity of Mary's Assumption (August 15) recalls Mary's entrance, body and soul, into heaven.

Mary's birthday is recalled on September 8. Her Presentation to God in the temple is remembered on November 21. The sorrows she endured are memorialized on September 15.

Particular devotions to Mary that have arisen over the centuries are also found in the Church's calendar: the Apparition of Mary at Lourdes in 1858 (February 11), the Feast of the Immaculate Heart of Mary (May 31), the Feast of Our Lady of Mount Carmel (July 16), and the Feast of the Queenship of Mary (August 22).

Devotion to Mary in the Church is not confined to a single day or a few special feast days. Through daily prayers and acts of piety, such as the Rosary, her memory is constantly evoked throughout the year. Hailed by the angel, "full of grace," she inspires the Church today, as she did the apostles, with a faithful love of her son, Jesus Christ.

St. Anthony was born in the village of Koman, Upper Egypt in 250. He was born into a wealthy Christian family, and when his parents died in 269, he and his sister were left alone.

About six months after his parents' deaths, while in church, he heard the words of the Gospel: "If you will be perfect, go sell all you have, and give to the poor; and come, follow me and you will have treasure in heaven."

Anthony felt as if God were speaking directly to him. He immediately left the church and gave all his property to the poor people of his village. Then, after providing for his sister, he left home to follow Christ.

He chose to live in a deserted place not far from Koman, where he devoted himself to prayer and work with his hands. He gave much of what he earned to the poor and kept only what he needed for his own support.

About 285, Anthony moved and settled on the top of a mountain where he lived in solitude for nearly twenty years. In the desert Anthony fought one of life's great battles—the battle with oneself. He faced his fears, his disappointments, his weariness, and his sins. Though the devil continually tempted him, Anthony became a stronger person.

French School. *St. Anthony Abbot,* (15th century)
York Museums Trust (York Art Gallery), UK

About 305, Anthony came down from the mountain and established the first Christian monastery at Fayum. In 311, during the Arian heresy, Anthony went to Alexandria to encourage the faithful. When the persecution abated, he established another monastery at Pispir, near the Nile River. In 312, he returned to a cave on Mt. Kolzim with his disciple, Macarius, and remained there for the rest of his life.

People from all over Egypt and throughout the world heard of this holy man living in the desert. Thousands of them came to his door to see him and ask his advice. Some adopted his life style and many became monks. As a result, Anthony is called the Father of Monasticism.

Everyone who met this shy, quiet man went away with a renewed desire to love God and live joyfully without fear.

In 355, Anthony returned to Alexandria to combat Arianism. He died in 356 on Mt. Kolzim.

ST. FRANCIS DE SALES

(1567-1622) bishop and doctor

St. Francis de Sales was born on August 21, 1567, at the Chateau de Sales in the kingdom of Savoy near Geneva, Switzerland. He came from a noble family and even as a child desired to serve God completely. Though frail and delicate, he had a quick, intelligent mind and a gentle, kind disposition. His family educated him at the best schools of his day.

In 1580, he entered the University of Paris and was drawn to the study of theology. He then attended the University of Padua, where he received his doctorate in law at the age of twenty-four.

His father wanted him to pursue a career in law and politics and enter into an advantageous marriage. But Francis wanted to be a priest. Against his father's wishes he was ordained in 1593 by the Bishop of Geneva.

The Catholic Church at that time was losing many of its people to the new churches of the Protestant Reformation. Francis set out to restore Catholicism in the region around Lake Geneva known as Chablais. Tirelessly and patiently preaching the ancient faith, writing leaflets that clearly explained the Catholic view, he gradually re-established a strong Catholicism in that area. In

Noel Halle. *St. Francois de Sales (1567-1622) Giving the Rule of the Visitation to St. Jeanne de Chantal (1572-1641), (1711-81)*
Eglise Saint-Louis-en-L'Ile, Paris, France

1602, he was appointed Bishop of Geneva.

From his residence at Annecy he organized his diocese and with a winning gentleness ministered to his people. His encouragement and wise counsel inspired many people to a better way of life. In 1608, his most famous book, An Introduction to a Devout Life, was published and soon circulated throughout the world. In 1610, he founded the Order of Visitation with St. Jane Frances de Chantal, whom he guided in the spiritual life.

Francis de Sales was convinced that God sees humanity as a great and varied garden, each person beautiful in his or her uniqueness. The various callings of life — soldier, prince, widow, married woman — are like the various flowers of the field; God loves them all. Through his or her own calling, each person can find a way to a deeper friendship with his or her creator. Francis approached people with genuine respect and gently guided them to recognize the unique path they would take in life. He made the journey to God joyful and possible for everyone to make. Above all, he advised against despair and the burden of fear.

He died at Lyons on December 28, 1622.

The Church celebrates the conversion of St. Paul because of its extraordinary nature. Paul, who was known as Saul before his conversion, was born at Tarsus in Cilicia, to Jewish parents. A Roman citizen, he was educated in Jerusalem under the tutelage of Gamaliel, a Pharisee. He became a Pharisee and fully embraced the law of Moses. Paul became an avowed enemy of the infant Church and engaged in the persecution of Christians. It is noted that he was present at the stoning death of St. Stephen.

Between the years 34 and 36, Paul was on his way to Damascus to arrest Christians and bring them back to Jerusalem. His encounter with Christ would change his life and have a dramatic effect on Christianity. Paul described what happened to the people of Jerusalem as he set out for Damascus.

"I set out with the intention of bringing the prisoners I would arrest back to Jerusalem for punishment. As I was traveling along, approaching Damascus around noon, a great light from the sky suddenly flashed all about me. I fell to the ground and heard a voice say to me, 'Saul, Saul, why do you persecute me?' I answered, 'Who are you, sir?' He said to

Michelangelo Merisi da Caravaggio. *The Conversion of St. Paul, 1601,*
(1571-1610) Santa Maria del Popolo, Rome, Italy

me, 'I am Jesus the Nazarene whom you are persecuting.' My companions saw the light but did not hear the voice speaking to me. 'What is it I must do, sir?' I asked, and the Lord replied, 'Get up and go to Damascus. There you will be told about everything you are destined to do.' But I could not see because of the brilliance of the light, I had to be taken by the hand and led into Damascus by my companions.

"A certain Ananias, a devout observer of the law and well spoken of by all the Jews who lived there, came and stood by me. 'Saul, my brother,' he said, 'recover your sight.' In that instant I regained my sight and looked at him. The next thing he said was, 'The God of our fathers long ago designated you to know his will, to look upon the Just One, and to hear the sound of his voice; before all men you are to be his witness to what you have seen and heard. Why delay, then? Be baptized at once and wash away your sins as you call upon his name.' "

Profoundly influenced by this grace of God, the converted apostle preached Christ to the nations. Today the feast of Paul's conversion ends the Church Unity Octave — an annual eight-day period of prayer for Christian unity. Inspired by Father Paul Wattson, founder of the Society of the

Atonement, this observance has spread from the United States to various other lands and is celebrated in many Protestant and Orthodox as well as Catholic churches.

ST. THOMAS AQUINAS

(1225-1274) priest and doctor

St. Thomas Aquinas, the great medieval Doctor of the Church, was born in the family castle of Rocco Secca in the town of Aquino, Italy, near the great abbey of Monte Cassino in 1225. His father, Landulf, was a nobleman and his mother, Theodora, was of Norman descent. As a boy of five he began his schooling at the Benedictine monastery at Monte Cassino. In 1239, he began studies at the University of Naples. There, Thomas became friendly with the Dominicans and wished to become a member of their community, but his family resisted his wishes. In 1244, his brother led a troop of soldiers and forced him back to the family castle where he was confined for two years. During that time, family members used every method to dissuade him from his goal, but Thomas remained firm, using the time to learn the Scriptures by heart and to study philosophy.

In 1245, his family permitted him to become a Dominican, and Thomas went to Cologne, Germany, to study under St. Albert the Great. His quiet, slow manner caused his companions to call him "the dumb ox," but soon they learned of his genius. "You call him a dumb ox," Albert told his students, "soon his voice will be heard through the world." He was ordained in Cologne about 1251

Sandro Botticelli. *St. Thomas Aquinas*, (1444/5-1510)
Abegg Collection, Riggisberg, Switzerland

and encouraged to return to Paris by Albert in 1252. He received his master of theology in 1256.

Thomas became one of the Church's great theologians and thinkers. Upon his return, he taught at the University of Paris. Between 1259 and 1268 he traveled extensively throughout Italy and taught in many of the small towns and villages.

In 1266, Thomas began his famous dissertation, the Summa Theologica. He returned to Paris in 1269 and became a confidant of Louis IX. Popes and kings, as well as scholars and students, sought his advice and wisdom.

In 1273, Thomas was unable to complete his masterpiece, the Summa Theologica. After a profound experience in prayer, he said to a companion, "All that I have written appears as so much straw compared to the things that have been revealed to me."

Toward the end of his life, someone saw him kneeling before a crucifix, hearing a voice from the cross say: "You have written well of me, Thomas; what reward do you want?" "Nothing but yourself, Lord," Thomas replied.

In 1274, Thomas was summoned by Pope Gregory X to attend the General Council at Lyons to reunite the Greek and Latin Churches. He died on the way at the Cistercian abbey of Fossa Nuova near Terracina, Italy, on March 7, 1274.

Francisco de Zurbaran. *St. Agatha, (1598-1664)*
Musee Fabre, Montpellier, France

FEBRUARY

ST. AGATHA   February 5
    (d. 251) virgin and martyr

St. Agatha, according to legend, was born into a wealthy and noble family in Catania, Sicily. During the persecution of Decius, Quintin, a Roman consul, desired her. Agatha refused his advances and was sent to a house of prostitution. She was repeatedly tortured and had her breasts cut off. Subjected to harsh torments, Agatha suffered death with courage and was united to Jesus Christ, her Lord, about 251.

Bulgarian School. *Icon of St. Cyril (826-69) and St. Methodius (c.815-85)*
Museum of History of Sofia, Sofia, Bulgaria

ST. CYRIL (825-869) monk February 14
    and
ST. METHODIUS (826-885) bishop

St. Cyril and St. Methodius were brothers born in Thessalonica, Greece. Cyril, who was baptized Constantine, assumed the name Cyril when he became a monk shortly before his death. He studied at the Imperial University in Constantinople under Photius. He was ordained soon after and became known as "the Philosopher." His brother, Methodius, served as governor of one of the Slav colonies in the Opsikion province. Afterwards he became a monk. In 861, at the request of Emperor Michael II, Cyril and Methodius went on a mission to convert the Khazars in Russia. The two embarked on missionary work that profoundly influenced the Slavic peoples of Eastern Europe.

In 862, Prince Rotislav of Moravia asked the Eastern Emperor for Christian missionaries to teach the Gospel to his people in their own language. Photius, now patriarch of Constantinople, assigned the task to Cyril and Methodius in 863. They prepared liturgical books and later translated the Scriptures into the Slavic language. They also provided an alphabet, known as the glagolithic alphabet, for their writing. Through their preaching and writing they brought Christianity to the countries of Bulgaria, Yugoslavia, and Russia.

Emperor Louis the German and missionaries from the Western Church questioned their methods. They sought, and eventually gained the approval of Pope Adrian II for their work. Pope Adrian II ordained them as bishops in 869. Cyril died in Rome on February 14, 869. His brother, Methodius, continued to labor as a missionary until his death on April 6, 885 in Velehrad, Czechoslovakia.

MARCH

ST. CASIMIR   March 4
  (1458-1484)

St. Casimir was born on October 3, 1458, at the royal palace in Cracow, Poland. He was the third of thirteen children of King Casimir IV of Poland and Elizabeth of Austria. Casimir was tutored by John Dlugosz and as a youth developed a deep friendship with God and devotion to Mary. In honor of Our Lady, Casimir frequently recited the Latin hymn, Omni die dic Mariae, which is also known as the Hymn of Casimir.

His desire to be poor in spirit like Jesus Christ prompted him to avoid the luxury of court life and its privileges. Instead, he preferred simple food and clothing and devoted his riches and influences to care for the poor people of Poland.

In 1471, his father sent him to lead an army into Hungary to overthrow King Matthias Corvinus. Casimir became convinced before the battle that the war was futile and unjust, so he ordered his soldiers home. Angered at his son, King Casimir IV had him imprisoned at his castle of Dobzki for three months. Casimir served as viceroy of Poland from 1479 to 1483. He had taken a vow of celibacy as a child, and despite pressure from his father, Casimir refused to marry the daughter of

Carlo Dolci. *St. Casimir (1458-84)*
Palazzo Pitti, Florence, Italy

Emperor Frederick III.

His integrity, fairness, and love for those in need deeply impressed the ruling class of Poland; his people called him "the Peacemaker" and patron of the poor. He died from lung disease at the age of twenty-five on March 4, 1484, and is buried at Vilna, Lithuania. Casimir is the patron of Poland and Lithuania.

Giovanni Battista Tiepolo. *Miracle of St. Patrick, c.1746,*
Museo Civico, Padua, Italy

(385-461) bishop

St. Patrick was born about 385 in either Dumbarton on the Clyde or Cumberland to the south of Hadrian's Wall. He was of Roman-British heritage and his father, Calpurnius, was a deacon and a municipal official. He was seized from his father's farm at age sixteen by Irish raiders who sold him into slavery in pagan Ireland. Six years later, he escaped and returned to his home. His captivity, however, had a deep religious effect on him and he longed to bring his Christian faith to the Irish people. In a dream, he heard "the voice of the Irish" calling him back.

Patrick studied at the monastery of Lérins, off the coast of France from 412 to 415. He spent his next fifteen years at Auxerre, France, and was probably ordained about 417 by St. Amator.

About 432, Patrick was appointed bishop by Germanus and went to Ireland to succeed Bishop Palladius. He went to the north and west of Ireland where the local Irish leaders welcomed him. Soon he established churches throughout the country and, though opposed fiercely by the pagan Druids, converted many. In 444, after visiting Rome, Patrick established his episcopal see in Armagh, which became the focal point of the Catholic Church's ministry in Ireland.

Patrick's own account of his conversion and missionary life is known as the Confessio. In it he saw himself as a humble instrument in God's hands, given gifts of wisdom and strength to bring an alien people to the true faith. "I am ready to give my life most willingly; to spend myself even to death in the country… Among this people I want to wait for the promise made by Christ in the Gospel, 'They shall come from the east and the west, and sit down with Abraham, Isaac and Jacob'."

Patrick died in 461 at Saul on Strangford Lough. He is the patron of Ireland.

(first century) husband of Mary

St. Joseph, husband of Mary and foster father of Jesus Christ, was a descendant of King David, according to the genealogy presented by the Gospel. Betrothed to Mary, he decided to divorce her quietly when he found she was with child, but an angel of the Lord told him to take her as his wife, since the child to be born was the "Holy One of God."

Joseph assisted at the birth of Jesus and became his support and guide through childhood. In a dream he was told by an angel to flee from Bethlehem with the infant and his mother, lest Herod kill the child. He accompanied them to the temple where Jesus was presented to God. With Mary, he sought the boy Jesus when he was lost on a pilgrimage to Jerusalem. In his work as a carpenter he shared the many hours of his trade with his young son.

Joseph, a man of faith, a just man, was a worthy successor to the great patriarchs — Abraham, Isaac, and Jacob. He followed the call of God through the mysterious circumstances that surrounded the coming of Jesus. God entrusted this silent, humble man with the unique privilege of raising his only Son as a growing child.

A saint close to God, he is honored as the patron of the universal Church.

Guido Reni. *St. Joseph and the Christ Child, 1634-40,* (1575-1642)
Museum of Fine Arts, Houston, Texas, USA

ST. VINCENT FERRER
(1350-1419) priest

April 5

St.Vincent was born at Valencia, Spain, in 1350. He joined the Dominicans in 1367, received further education in Barcelona and Toulouse, and became known as a famous preacher. Vincent became heavily involved in the "great schism," when rival Popes were reigning in Rome and Avignon from 1378 to 1409.

In 1379, Vincent became a member of the court of Cardinal Peter de Luna, who was a supporter of Clement VII of Avignon. When Clement died, Cardinal Peter de Luna was named his successor and became known as Benedict XIII. After his election, Vincent was summoned to Avignon in 1394 and became Benedict's confessor. At first, Vincent strongly believed that the seat of the Church was in Avignon. However, he had a vision which changed his life and convinced him that Benedict's reign was only hurting the Church.

In 1399, Benedict gave Vincent permission to leave Avignon for the purpose of preaching. As a preacher of the Gospel, he moved the hearts and stirred the minds of people throughout Europe, as well as Spain. According to witnesses, his words, eloquent and simple, spoken from a loving

Gasparo Diziani. *St. Vincent Ferrer performing a miracle*,
Private Collection, Bonhams, London, UK

conviction, were understood by everyone he addressed, even though they spoke a different language. Great crowds flocked to hear him speak of Christ's judgment, and those who listened were moved to change their lives and turn from their sins.

In 1414, the Council of Constance demanded that Benedict XIII resign his papacy in order to unify the Church, but Benedict refused. In 1416, Vincent advised King Ferdinand of Aragon to withdraw his support of Benedict. When this happened, Benedict XIII was deposed and the "great schism" had ended. Vincent died three years later in 1419, while preaching in France during Holy Week.

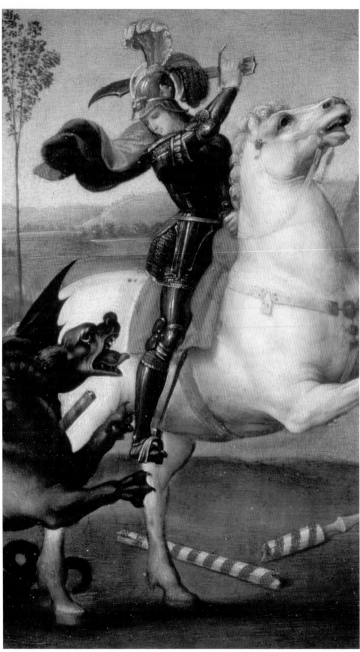

Raphael (Raffaello Sanzio of Urbino). *St. George Struggling with the Dragon*, (1483-1520) Louvre, Paris, France

ST. GEORGE

(fourth century) martyr

Historically, very little is know of St. George's life. According to tradition, he was a Christian soldier who suffered martyrdom about the year 303 in Palestine, sometime before the reign of Emperor Constantine. A legend beginning in the twelfth century and later popularized in the thirteenth century by a book called The Golden Legend tells of George as a Christian soldier born in Cappadocia. In Sylene, Libya, he rescued the king's daughter from a dragon and in turn killed it. As a result, thousands of people were baptized and led to God.

Devotion to George spread to the West during the Crusades when he was invoked for protection by King Richard I of England and his army. St. George is the patron saint of England as well as Portugal, Germany, Aragon, Genoa, and Venice.

(first century) evangelist

St. Mark, author of the second Gospel, was a member of the early Christian community at Jerusalem. St. Paul and St. Barnabas, his cousin, took him on their first missionary journey. When they reached Cyprus, however, Mark left them to return to Jerusalem, perhaps because he missed home. This caused Paul to question for a while Mark's reliability as a missionary, and the incident brought about a disagreement between him and Barnabas. Later, Mark became Paul's trusted companion at Rome, during one of Paul's imprisionments. He was also an associate of Peter.

One tradition relates that Mark became Bishop of Alexandria in Egypt. Around the ninth century, his relics were brought to Venice where they rest in the great Cathedral of San Marco.

Mark is depicted in art as a winged lion, probably suggested by the description in his Gospel of John the Baptist as "a voice crying in the desert." It is believed that he wrote his Gospel between 60 and 70 A.D.

Jacopo (Il Vecchio) Palma. *St. Mark,* (c.1480-1528)
York Museums Trust (York Art Gallery), UK

Carlo Dolci. *St. Catherine of Siena*, (1616-86)
Dulwich Picture Gallery, London, UK

(1347-1380) virgin and doctor

The youngest of twenty-five children, St. Catherine was born at Siena, Italy, in 1347 to a wealthy businessman, Giacomo Benincasa and his wife, Lapa. As a young girl of six, while walking home one day, she had a remarkable vision of Jesus. Seated in glory with Sts. Peter, Paul, and John, he smiled upon her. From that time on, Catherine wished to give herself to prayer and the service of God.

Her parents, wishing her married with all the advantages they could give her, at first tried to prevent her. Finally they realized that God had favored her and Catherine became a Dominican tertiary at the age of sixteen. She lived at home while following the rule recommended for those seeking God.

She began to nurse the sick in the Siena hospitals, preferring cancer patients and lepers whom others found too difficult to care for. In a vision, Jesus told her, "I desire to come closer to you through the love you have for your neighbor." Gradually, a number of companions were drawn to her to share her inspiration and work. When an epidemic of plague broke out, a friend wrote, "She was always with the plague-stricken. She prepared them for death, she buried them with her own hands. I myself witnessed the joy with which she nursed them and how effective her words were." Frequently, Catherine went to the prisons to counsel those condemned to death and prepare them for their final ordeal.

Her reputation for holiness and wisdom spread not only in Siena, but also in the neighboring cities of Pisa, Lucca, and Florence. Families and rival political parties called on her to mediate their disputes and reconcile their differences.

While on a trip to Pisa in 1375, Catherine received the stigmata. In 1376, she went to Avignon, France, to mediate the armed conflict between Florence and the papal government, but her efforts failed. More important, she was able to convince Pope Gregory XI to return to Rome for the good of the Church. When he died, Pope Urban VI was elected in Rome and a rival Pope, Clement VII, was installed in Avignon. This is considered to be the beginning of the "great schism." Catherine went to Rome in 1378 to try and end the dispute, as she was a staunch defender of Pope Urban VI. She died in Rome honored for her sanctity on April 29, 1380, at the age of thirty-three. She is a Doctor of the Church.

MAY

ST. PHILIP (first century)   May 3
    and
ST. JAMES (d. 62) apostles

St. Philip was born at Bethsaida in Galilee. He was one of the apostles and a disciple of John the Baptist. Philip heard the call of Jesus, "Follow me," and accompanied Jesus on his public ministry. He is mentioned in St. John's Gospel, and invited the apostle Bartholomew to come and see Christ. At the Last Supper, he said to Jesus, "Lord, show us the Father, and it is enough."

According to tradition, Philip was present with the apostles who spent ten days waiting in the upper room in Jerusalem for the coming of the Holy Spirit at Pentecost. After the death of Christ, Philip preached the Gospel in Phrygia, Asia Minor. He was martyred at Hierapolis by soldiers loyal to Emperor Domitian.

St. James, also known as James the Less, was one of the twelve apostles and is called "the son of Alpheus" and "the brother of the Lord" in the Gospels. It is assumed, however, that he was most likely a cousin of Jesus. He is believed to be the author of the Epistle of St. James in the New Testament.

James was appointed the Bishop of Jerusalem

Peter Paul Rubens. *St. James the Apostle,* (1577-1640)
Prado, Madrid, Spain

and was present at the Council of Jerusalem. He was also present with the apostles in the upper room awaiting the coming of the Holy Spirit at Pentecost. James remained in Jerusalem after Pentecost and was stoned to death there in 62.

ST. GREGORY VII   May 25
(1028-1085) pope

St. Gregory VII was born in Tuscany, Italy, in 1208 and baptized Hildebrand. He was educated at a monastery in Rome and became a monk at Cluny in 1047. He served faithfully in the administration of the Church as secretary to Pope Gregory VI and counselor to Pope Leo IX. Pope Alexander II died in 1073 and Hildebrand was elected to succeed him.

As Pope Gregory VII, he sought the reforms of the Church which had begun with Pope Leo IX. At that time, the church suffered from simony, lay investiture, and marriage of the clergy. Many secular rulers controlled the appointment of bishops and other Church officials within their lands. Often their appointments were unqualified or unworthy, with the result that the Church's religious life was seriously harmed.

Gregory's demand that the Church alone should appoint its bishops brought him into conflict with the kings and rulers of Europe, especially Emperor Henry IV of Germany, all of whom were in favor of lay investiture. Because of his beliefs, Henry was excommunicated by Pope Gregory. In 1077, fearlessly for his political future because of being excommunicated, Henry went to Conossa, Italy, to beg Gregory's pardon which was granted.

However, the struggle for the power of appointment continued through Pope Gregory's reign. Henry invaded Italy in 1084 and vanquished Rome. He installed an anti-pope, Clement III, and banished Pope Gregory. Gregory was saved by Robert Guiscard, Dule of Normany, but still had to leave Rome. He died in exile in Salerno on may 25, 1085. His last words were, "I have loved right and hated evil, so I die in exile."

Andrea Sacchi. *St. Gregory,* (1599-1661)
Burghley House Collection, Lincolnshire, UK

Jean Auguste Dominique Ingres. *Joan of Arc at the Coronation of King Charles VII*, (1780-1867) Louvre, Paris, France

ST. JOAN OF ARC
(1412-1431) virgin

St. Joan of Arc, patron saint of France, was born into the peasant class in the first month of 1412. Her parents worked the land and raised the usual collection of farm animals. As other young girls of her age would customarily do, she looked after the family sheep and cattle. From one perspective, her world was probably best defined by two words, obedience and loyalty, and both words applicably described a peasant's relationship to both civil and Church authority. Her world was also a world at war. For decades a state of war had existed between England and what was then the disjointed country of France.

Even from early childhood, Joan was naturally inclined to a life of religious devotion, and thus her admission to be the recipient of celestial revelations drew little attention from those aware of her claim. However, in her eighteenth year, when she announced that God had personally called her to intervene in the war between France and England, some people did take notice, and most notably the man who would in a matter of months be crowned King of France, Charles VII.

When Joan first sought an audience with Charles to discuss what God wanted her to do, her request was not looked upon with much seriousness. But finally, after satisfying both religious authorities and civil advisors, Joan was granted an opportunity to plead her cause. After making a favorable impression on Charles, Joan was given command of a small army, and beginning on May 8, of 1429, she turned the tide of battle in favor of the French crown, thus allowing Charles to be formally installed as Charles VII, King of France.

Unfortunately, Joan's fame and glory were short lived. After being taken prisoner by enemy troops, she was eventually sold to the English who had her tried as both a heretic and a witch. For all practical purposes, the eventual outcome of her trial was known from the start. She was to be found guilty of the trumpeted-up charges leveled against her, and because of their perceived seriousness, the punishment would be death. There was no surprise when on May 30, 1431, Joan of Arc was burned at the stake. Her ashes were subsequently thrown into the Seine to assure any remembrance of who she was would be quickly forgotten.

That, however, was not to be the case. A quarter of a century later her family appealed for a new hearing of the evidence which condemned Joan to such an early and horrible death. Pope Calixtus III himself announced a reversal of the original verdict, although centuries would pass before Joan was eventually universally recognized for the saint she truly was. On May 13, 1920, Pope Benedict XV solemnly proclaimed Joan to be a canonized saint in the Catholic Church.

JUNE

ST. ANTHONY OF PADUA   June 13
(1195-1231) priest and doctor

St. Anthony of Padua was born at Lisbon, Portugal, in 1195. His surname comes from the Italian city where he lived the latter part of his life. His parents were members of the Portuguese nobility; his father was a knight at the court of King Alfonso II.

His early education took place at the cathedral of Lisbon. At the age of fifteen, he joined the Regular Canons of St. Augustine and was transferred to the monastery at Coimbra two years later because of distractions caused by his friends' visits. At the monastery, Anthony devoted himself to prayer and study and became a learned scholar of the Bible.

In 1220, Don Pedro of Portugal brought the relics of Franciscans who had been martyred to Coimbra. This had a tremendous effect on Anthony, who requested admission to the Franciscans. In 1221, he was accepted. Soon after, he set out for Morocco to preach the Gospel to the Moors. On the way to Morocco, he was forced to return to Europe because of illness. On his return home, a storm drove his ship to the shores of Italy, where he would live the rest of his life.

Upon his return, Anthony went to Assisi, where the general chapter meeting of 1221 took place. At the meeting, he was assigned to the hermitage of San Paolo near Forli. It was in Forli that he gave a great sermon which propelled him into his calling as a preacher.

A gifted preacher, Anthony was also called upon to teach theology to his fellow Franciscans. He was the first member of the Franciscans to be so honored. Anthony drew large crowds wherever he went in Italy, but his greatest success was in Padua where the entire city flocked to hear his word and welcomed him as another St. Francis.

After the death of Francis, Anthony became the minister provincial of Emilia or Romagna. In 1226, he was elected as the envoy from the general chapter to Pope Gregory IX. Soon after, he was released from this duty so he could continue his preaching. He returned to Padua, where he preached until his death. Anthony died on June 13, 1231, at the age of thirty-six. He is a Doctor of the Church.

Francisco de Zurbaran. *St. Anthony of Padua*, (1598-1664)
Prado, Madrid, Spain

Giovanni Battista Tiepolo. *St. Aloysius Gonzaga in Glory, c.1726,*
Samuel Courtauld Trust, Courtauld Institute of Art Gallery

ST. ALOYSIUS GONZAGA

(1568-1591) religious

St. Aloysius Gonzaga was born in the castle of Castiglione delle Stivieri in Lombardy, Italy, on March 9, 1568. His father, Ferrante, was the Marquis of Castiglione and held a high position in the court of King Philip II of Spain. He wanted Aloysius to be a great soldier, but Aloysius had other desires; he wanted to serve God with his body and soul.

In 1577, Aloysius and his brother, Ridolfo, went to Florence to learn Latin and Italian. In 1579, they were placed in the court of the Duke of Mantua, and their father was appointed governor of Montserrat. At the age of twelve, Aloysius was afflicted with a kidney disease which would bother him for the rest of his life.

About this time, Aloysius read a book about Jesuit missionaries in India and became greatly intrigued with the idea of joining the Society of Jesus. He began to live as a monk in the winters at Casale-Monferrato and taught catechism to the poor boys of Castiglione in the summer. In 1581, his father was called to accompany Empress Mary of Austria on her trip from Bohemia to Spain. The family moved to Spain, and Aloysius and his brother were made pages in the court of Prince Don Diego.

Still true to his calling, Aloysius desired to become a Jesuit, but his family would not hear of it. In time, his father capitulated to his desires and Aloysius entered the Jesuit novitiate in Rome in 1585. He went to Milan to study, became a novice, and made his vows in 1587. In 1591, an epidemic broke out in Rome. The Jesuits opened a hospital of their own and Aloysius worked there to help victims of the plague. Aloysius caught the plague, and when told that he had contracted it, he cried out, "I rejoiced when I heard them say: we will go to God's house." To his mother he wrote: "Our parting will not be for long; we shall see each other again in heaven; we shall be united with our Savior..." After receiving viaticum and the last rites from his confessor, St. Robert Bellarmine, Aloysius died on June 21, 1591.

ST. THOMAS MORE   June 22
(1478-1535) martyr

St. Thomas More was born in London, England, in 1478. He went to Oxford, studied law, and received his doctorate in 1504. He entered the English Parliament in 1504. He married Jane Holt in 1505 and had four children: Margaret, Elizabeth, Cecilia, and John.

The More household was a model of spiritual and intellectual life. Thomas saw that his daughters were well educated—something unusual in those days—and led his family in prayer, reading the Scriptures, and discussion on the important matters of his day. He welcomed into his home not only famous scholars, like St. John Fisher and Erasmus, but also his poorer neighbors, whom he treated warmly and respectfully. When Jane died, Thomas married Alice Middleton, a widow, in 1511.

When Henry VIII became king, he sought out More as a friend and advisor. In 1529, Thomas became Lord Chancellor of England and functioned wisely and justly in that office. His friend, Erasmus, wrote: "In serious matters no man is more prized, while if the king wishes to relax no one's conversation is more cheerful … Happy the nation where kings appoint such officials."

Shortly after Thomas took office, Henry VIII

Hans the Younger Holbein. *Portrait of Sir Thomas More (1478-1535)*, Private Collection/ © Philip Mould, Historical Portraits Ltd, UK

began proceedings to divorce Catherine of Aragon. Because he could not agree with the king, Thomas kept silent and eventually in 1532, he resigned his office.

Without income and in disfavor, he spent the next few years writing and reflecting, living quietly with his family, "being merry together," as he said. But in 1534, he was asked, with John Fisher, to take an oath to the king that he could not accept. He refused and, after fifteen months in prison, he was beheaded on July 6, 1535, "the king's good servant but God's first." He is the patron of lawyers.

In prison he wrote to his daughter, "I trust only in God's merciful goodness. His grace has strengthened me till now and made me content to lose goods, land, and life as well, rather than swear against my conscience. I will not mistrust him, Meg, though I shall feel myself weakening and being overcome with fear. I shall remember how St. Peter at a blast of wind began to sink because of his lack of faith, and I shall do as he did: call upon Christ and pray to him for help. And then I trust he shall place his holy hand on me and in the stormy seas hold me up from drowning."

The birthday of John the Baptist, six months before the birth of Jesus, has been celebrated on June 24 from the earliest days of the Church. Jesus himself called John, who prepared the way for him by his preaching, the greatest of men. A "voice in the desert," John, as the final prophet of the Old Testament, told the people of his time that their Lord was near.

The announcement of John's birth by the Angel Gabriel to Zachary, his father, was received with disbelief because Zachary's wife, Elizabeth, was beyond childbearing age. Yet the angel insisted, "You shall call his name John for he will be great before the Lord and filled with the Holy Spirit, even from his mother's womb."

In the wastelands of Judea, people from all ranks of society — soldiers and priests, tax collectors and workers — came to hear John and their hearts were moved by his call to repent. Many were baptized by him in the River Jordan as a sign of their conversion; some remained to live with him as his disciples. His denunciation of King Herod's immoral conduct shocked the king's court, and John eventually suffered death for speaking truth to power.

Jesus began his own mission by being baptized by John. Recognizing the Son of God,

Alessandro Allori. *The Baptism of Christ*, (1535-1607)
Galleria dell' Accademia, Florence, Italy

whose "sandals he was not worthy to untie," John said, "He must increase, and I must decrease." John's life prepared for Jesus who was eternal life. Early commentators never failed to note that after June 24, the feast of John the Baptist, the sun's light begins to decrease until December 25, the birth of Jesus, when the light of the sun increases again.

ST. PETER (d. 64)   June 29
     and
ST. PAUL (d. 64) apostles

A feast honoring these two great saints has been celebrated by the Roman Catholic Church since the third century. There is sound evidence that both Sts. Peter and Paul preached in the city of Rome and were martyred there under the Emperor Nero about the year 64. The Church of Rome praises them as its founding apostles: "Peter, our leader in faith, and Paul, its fearless preacher. Peter raised up the Church from the faithful flock of Israel, Paul brought God's call to the nations." (Preface from the Mass)

Simon, a fisherman on the Sea of Galilee, was one of the first whom Jesus called to follow him. Changing his name to Peter, "Rock," the Lord promised to build his Church on him and gave him power in heaven and on earth. A natural spokesman for the other disciples, Peter called Jesus "the Christ, the Son of the living God."

When Jesus was arrested, Peter denied him three times and afterwards wept bitterly over his enormous betrayal of the one he promised to die for. When he rose from the dead, Jesus asked Peter three times if he loved him and, hearing the disciple's simple answer, "Yes, Lord, you know I love you," gave him again a privileged place at his side. "Come, follow me."

Filled with the Holy Spirit at Pentecost, Peter

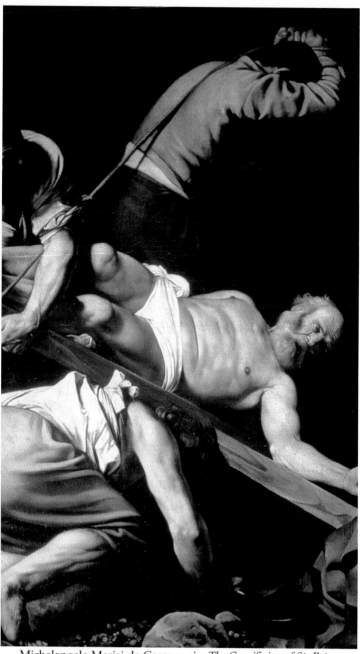

Michelangelo Merisi da Caravaggio. *The Crucifixion of St. Peter,*
(1571-1610) Santa Maria del Popolo, Rome, Italy

began to preach about Jesus Christ to the crowds in Jerusalem and Samaria and later made his way to Rome where he died a martyr's death as leader of that Church. Tradition says he died crucified head down, since he considered himself unworthy to die as his Lord had done.

Saul of Tarsus was a zealous Jew, a Pharisee, who after his dramatic conversion on the way to the city of Damascus became a fervent apostle of Jesus. After a three-year period in Arabia, where he assimilated his new faith, Paul journeyed to the cities of Damascus, Jerusalem, Antioch, and then crisscrossed the cities of Asia Minor establishing communities of Christians among the gentiles. Because of his activity he suffered constant harassment from his enemies, enduring shipwreck, imprisonment, and beatings. At the same time he was greatly loved by those Christians to whom he ministered; Corinthians, Ephesians, Galatians, Romans. To them St. Paul wrote his powerful letters of consolation and instruction which the Church still reads today as inspired by God himself.

After imprisonment in Rome, he was beheaded along the Ostian Way where his burial place is still venerated. In his letter to Timothy he wrote, "The time has come for me to go. I have fought the good fight; I have run the race: I have kept the faith. Now I await the crown of Justice which the Lord, the just judge, will give me on that day, and not only to me but to all who long for his coming."

Bernardo Strozzi. *The Incredulity of St. Thomas,* (1581-1644)
Museo de Arte, Ponce, Puerto Rico, West Indies

JULY

    (first century) apostle

St. Thomas, one of the twelve apostles, was a Jew from Galilee called by Jesus to accompany him on his mission to proclaim the Kingdom of God. When Jesus' life was threatened as he went to raise Lazarus from the dead, Thomas said to the others, "Let us also go, that we may die with him." At the Last Supper, when Jesus spoke of going away to his Father, Thomas replied, "Lord, we do not know where you are going, and how can we know the way?" With the rest of the apostles, Thomas fled when Jesus was arrested and put to death.

On Easter Sunday, Thomas was not with the others when Jesus came into the room where they were. Though they told him jubilantly, "We have seen the Lord!" Thomas answered, "I will not believe until I put my finger into the nail marks in his hands and his side." The expression "doubting Thomas" comes from this incident.

One week later, when Jesus appeared again to his disciples, Thomas was with them. Jesus said, "Take your finger and examine my hands. Put your hand into my side. Do not remain an unbeliever. Believe!" Thomas said, "My Lord and my God!"

"The unbelief of Thomas has done more for our

faith than the faith of the other disciples," St. Gregory the Great has said. Our doubts are answered by the demand of Thomas to know that Jesus' resurrection was real.

Thomas is said to have preached the Gospel to the people of India. He was martyred eight miles from Madras and buried at Mylapore, India. The date of his death is unknown.

   (480-547) abbot

St. Benedict, brother of St. Scholastica, was born at Nursia, Italy, in 480. His family was wealthy, and he was educated in Rome at a time when barbarian invasions and moral decline seriously threatened to destroy the city and the Roman empire. Disgusted with the moral decline of his companions and society in general, Benedict left Rome and lived in the village of Enfide for a number of years.

About 500, Benedict went to the wild and remote area of Subiaco. While there, he came under the tutelage of the monk, Romanus. Benedict became a monk and spent the next three years living a life of prayer and solitude in a cave. He began to attract many followers, and by 525, he had founded twelve monasteries in Subiaco.

In 529, after this was accomplished, Benedict left for Monte Cassino. Again, many disciples were drawn to him. In 530, he founded the great monastery at Monte Cassino which would become the focal point for Western monasticism. Benedict became the abbot of Monte Cassino and organized his companions into one monastic community. The Benedictine Rule inspired monastic life in the Western Church for centuries to come.

Monasticism and its monasteries were instrumental in preserving Western civilization in modern Europe and the West. A wise spiritual leader and worker of miracles, Benedict's life and works profoundly affected the spirituality and life of the Church and Western civilization. He died at Monte Cassino on March 21, 547.

Pietro Perugino. *St. Benedict*, (c.1445-1523)
Vatican Museums and Galleries, Vatican City, Italy

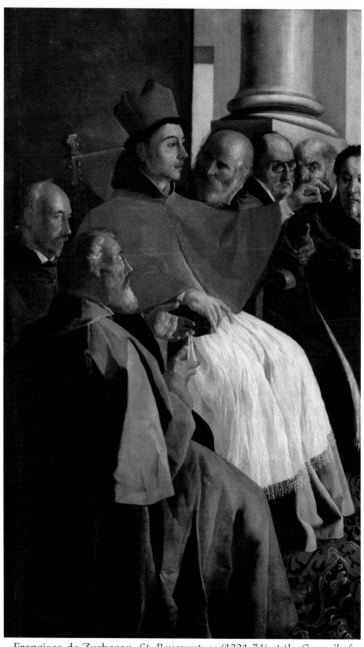

Francisco de Zurbaran. *St. Bonaventure (1221-74) at the Council of Lyons in 1274, 1627, (1598-1664)*
Louvre, Paris, France

ST. BONAVENTURE
(1218-1274) bishop and doctor

St. Bonaventure was born at Bagnorea, near Viterbo, Italy, in 1218. He became a Franciscan and studied at the University of Paris under a brilliant Englishman, Alexander of Hales. Bonaventure, also known as the "Seraphic Doctor," began an outstanding career as a teacher of theology and Holy Scripture at the University of Paris between 1248 and 1257. With St. Thomas Aquinas, his good friend, Bonaventure received his doctorate in theology in 1257 from the University of Paris.

That same year, Bonaventure was chosen minister general of the Franciscans. In 1265, Pope Clement IV wanted him to become Archbishop of York, but he declined. However, in 1273, Pope Gregory X appointed him Cardinal-Bishop of Albany.

Some of the great writings of St. Bonaventure are Commentary on the Sentences, The Perils of the Last Times, Concerning the Poverty of Christ, and Concerning Perfection of Life. Bonaventure not only enlightened the minds of those he taught, but also stirred their hearts. Though he searched into the depths of knowledge, he knew the importance of ordinary life. One becomes holy only by "doing common things well and being constantly faithful to small things." A constant joy seemed to fill this genuine flower of St. Francis. As he himself said, "Joy is the great sign of God's grace within the soul." He died while taking part in the Council of Lyons on July 15, 1274. St. Bonaventure is a Doctor of the Church.

ST. MARY MAGDALENE

(first century)

St. Mary Magdalene is one of the most appealing characters in the Gospels. Only a few details about her appear there, yet Christians know her as a woman of great love, desire, and unwavering loyalty. She was born at Mandala, near Tiberias, in Galilee.

Mary Magdalene stood beside Jesus while he was dying on the Cross. With Mary, his mother, and a few other disciples, she watched helplessly as the one she loved suffered through the dark hours of Good Friday. Then with the others she prepared his dead body for burial.

Early Easter morning, she returned anxiously to his tomb to complete the burial anointings, only to find his body gone. She began to weep. Through her tears she suddenly saw a man standing beside her whom she thought was the gardener. When he spoke her name, she knew he was Jesus, risen from the dead.

"Mary!" Jesus said to her. "Rabboni! Teacher!" Mary joyfully responded. Then Jesus spoke these mysterious words, "Do not cling to me, for I have not yet ascended to the Father."

We can see Jesus, not rejecting her at this joyous moment, but readying her, who followed him so devotedly in life, for following him now in

Pietro Perugino. *St. Mary Magdalene,* (c.1469-1523) (after)
Palazzo Pitti, Florence, Italy

faith. Reach out and cling to me now by faith, he seems to say. Touch me with the hand of your faith; seek me with eyes of faith; run towards me with limbs of faith. Now I will never be far from you. I am forever in your heart.

"I have seen the Lord," Mary announced to Jesus' disciples. Her experiences of the Lord, in his ministry, in the desolate hours on Calvary, in the brightening hours of Easter morning, echo through the centuries to strengthen our faith. She loved much, and through her love she found the God she sought.

STS. JOACHIM and ANN
parents of Mary

Ancient Christian tradition records the names of Sts. Joachim and Ann as the parents of Mary, the mother of Jesus. They were both members of the tribe of Judah of the house of David. According to tradition, Joachim and Ann came to Jerusalem from Galilee. Over the centuries, they have been honored, especially in the East, at great churches and shrines built in memory of them. Historically and biblically, not much is known of Joachim and Ann, except that they are the parents of Mary and grandparents of Jesus.

By their fruits we know how people lived, Jesus taught. The Church recognizes the grandparents of Jesus as models of family virtue and faith, which they transmitted to their offspring.

Ubaldo Gandolfi. *The Visitation*, (1728-81)
Private Collection, Bonhams, London, UK

French School. *Saint Ignatius of Loyola, (17th century)*
Chateau de Versailles, France

ST. IGNATIUS LOYOLA   July 31
(1491-1556) priest

Founder of the Society of Jesus, St. Ignatius Loyola was born in the castle of Loyola at Azpetia in Guipuzcoa, Spain, in 1491. His father, Don Beltran, was lord of Oñaz and Loyola and head of one of the most ancient and noble families of Spain. Ignatius, christened Iñigo, was the youngest of eleven children. He became a page at the court of King Ferdinand V of Aragon, and entered the military under the command of the Duke of Nagara.

In 1521, a cannon ball broke his right shin and tore open his left calf during the battle of Pamplona against France. After being wounded, he was returned to the family castle at Loyola to recuperate. While recovering, he read books about the life of Christ and the lives of the saints. He was so inspired by what he had read, that he decided to dedicate his life to Christ. After his recovery, Ignatius made a pilgrimage to the Shrine of Our Lady at Montserrat. For the next two years, he spent time in Manresa, alternating between a pauper's hospice and a cove. It was during this two-year period of prayer and solitude that he began his great book Spiritual Exercises.

Ignatius left Manresa in 1523 and went to the Holy Land. He returned to Spain in 1524 and went to Barcelona to study Latin. In 1526, he entered the University of Alcala. He went to Paris in 1528 and in 1534, at the age of forty-three, received his master of arts degree. While Ignatius was a student in Paris, he became very friendly with six fellow divinity students, one of whom was St. Francis Xavier.

In 1534, Ignatius and his six companions took a vow of chastity and poverty in a chapel on Montmartre. They pledged to preach the Gospel in Palestine and to offer their services directly to Pope Paul III. This is considered to be the founding of the Society of Jesus, or the Jesuits, as they are commonly known.

In 1537, Ignatius and his companions, who now numbered nine, went to Venice and were ordained. As they could not go to the Holy Land, they made a trip to Rome to offer their services directly to Pope Paul III. Thus, the Order was officially recognized by Pope Paul III in a papal bull on September 27, 1540.

Ignatius was chosen the first superior general, and the members of the Order made their final vows in 1541. Ignatius spent the rest of his life in Rome directing the activities of the Society of Jesus. His book, Spiritual Exercises, was published in 1548. He died in Rome on July 31, 1556.

AUGUST

August 8
(1170-1221) priest

St. Dominic was born at Calaruega, in Castile, Spain, in 1170. While a student in Palencia, he became a canon of the Cathedral of Orma. After his ordination, he joined the chapter, which adhered to the Rule of St. Augustine. In 1210, he became prior of the chapter.

In 1204, King Alfonso IX of Castile asked Bishop Diego d'Azevedo of Osma to perform he marriage of his son in Denmark. Dominic accompanied the bishop, and during their journey through France they went through Languedoc where they were confronted with the heresy of the Albigenses, a group of teachers who had become influential in certain parts of the country. While in Albigenses, Dominic met a man who was deeply confused by the Albigenses. Dominic spent the whole night in discussion with him and by daybreak the man was confirmed once again in his Catholic faith.

From this meeting, Dominic clearly saw his own mission: to preach the Gospel of Christ, battle the heresy of the Albigenses, and gather around him a group of holy and learned teachers who would instruct those in error. He remained in

Don Juan Carreno de Miranda. *St. Dominic*, (1614-85)
Museum of Fine Arts, Budapest, Hungary

Albigenses for nearly ten years, preaching the word of God. In 1206, he founded a convent in Prouille.

In 1214, Dominic moved to Toulouse, received an endowment, and attended the Fourth Lateran Council in 1215. In 1216, Dominic gathered his sixteen companions in Prouille and adopted by-laws for his congregation, which became known as the Order of preachers, or the Dominicans. These dedicated men and women combined learning with holiness and simplicity of life in the mission to spread the truth of Christ in the battle against the Albigenses. Pope Honorius III approved the congregation in 1216 and Toulouse became its headquarters.

Soon after, the friars were sent in all directions. Friaries would be established in Spain, France, England, and Italy. Dominic was appointed master general of the order in 1220 by Pope Honorius III and held the first general chapter of the Order in Bologna that same year. He died at Bologna on August 6, 1221.

ST. CLARE

(1193-1253) religious

St. Clare was born at Assisi, Italy, in 1193. When she was eighteen, St. Francis was preaching in Assisi and his words greatly inspired her. In 1212, on Palm Sunday, she ran away from home and went to Portiuncula, where Francis lived. He met her at the chapel of Our Lady of the Angels, cut off her hair, and gave her a sackcloth held together by a cord. She went to live in the Benedictine convent of St. Paul near Bastia.

Her family greatly objected, but their objections fell on deaf ears. Clare moved to a convent in Sant' Angelo di Panzo and was joined by her sister who was fifteen. In 1215, Clare, along with her sister, mother, and other companions, went to live in a convent associated with the Church of San Damiano, outside Assisi. Clare was appointed superior of the congregation by St. Francis, and this is considered to be the origin of the Poor Clares. In a short time, convents were opened in Italy, France, Germany, and Prague.

The Poor Clares adopted a severe life of poverty, silence, and austerity. They did not own any property or possessions and existed only on contributions. In 1228, Pope Gregory IX granted them the privilegium paupertatis, which excused them from having any material possessions.

Clare was superior of the order for over forty years. She died at the convent of San Damiano in 1253.

Don Juan Carreno de Miranda.
St. Clare Receiving the Veil from St. Francis of Assisi,
Italian School, Musee des Beaux-Arts, Caen, France

Alonso Cano. *St. Bernard and the Virgin*, (1601-67)
Prado, Madrid, Spain

ST. BERNARD

(1090-1153) abbot and doctor

St. Bernard was born at Fontaines, a castle near Dijon, France, in 1090. His was a wealthy and noble family and his father, Tescelin Sorrel, was a Burgundian noble. Bernard was well educated and sent to Chântillon on the Seine for a complete education among the secular canons.

His mother, whom he loved dearly, died when Bernard was a young man. Deeply touched by her death and with a growing love for God, Bernard entered the Cistercians at Citeaux in 1112. He was joined by thirty-one companions, including four of his brothers and an uncle. The abbot of Citeaux, St. Stephen, sent Bernard with twelve companions, to establish a new monastery in the diocese of Langres in Champagne. In time, Bernard was chosen as the abbot of the monastery of Clairvaux, from which sixty-eight new monasteries were founded throughout Europe by the time of his death.

As a monk, Bernard worked tirelessly to strengthen religious life, His sermons and writings, especially De Diligendo Deo and De Consideratione, describing the workings of God with the human soul, inspired the people of his time. They were the result of Bernard's own experience of God's grace in his life.

The needs of the Church and his society

continually called this eloquent saint from his monastery. Popes, bishops, and princes sought his advice in matters of policy and politics. He always sought to keep the Christian faith uncompromised.

In the disputed papal election of 1130, Bernard supported Pope Innocent II against the claims of the antipope Anacletus II. In 1145, the papal legate, Cardinal Alberic, asked Bernard to go to Languedoc to preach against the heresy of the Albigenses.

In 1145, Pope Eugenius III, the successor to Pope Innocent II, had been the abbot of the Cistercian monastery of Tre Fontane. He asked Bernard to preach in France and Germany to generate enthusiasm for a Second Crusade. The Crusade was a failure and Bernard had to endure much criticism.

The hearts of men and women throughout Europe were stirred by the faith and eloquence of this dynamic saint. His great prayers to Mary, the Mother of God — for example, his "Memorare" — are witness to his strong devotion to her as well as her Son. He died at Clairvaux on August 20, 1153. Bernard is a Doctor of the Church.

ST. ROSE OF LIMA
(1586-1617) virgin

St. Rose was born at Lima Peru, in 1586. She was confirmed by St. Turibius, Archbishop of Lima, and took the name Rose, as Isabel was her baptized name. Despite objections from her parents and friends, Rose admired St. Catherine of Siena, and was attracted to a life of prayer and reflection.

Her parents fell on hard times and Rose worked in the garden all day and sewed at night. She was very happy with this way of life, but her parents wanted her to marry. She refused their wishes, took a vow of virginity, and entered the Third Order of St. Dominic at the age of twenty. She became a recluse and lived in a small hut in the garden. She even went so far as to wear a thin crown of silver lined with sharp studs, a modern-day crown of thorns.

St. Rose cared for poor children, slaves, Indians and elderly people in an infirmary she set up in her family home. This is considered to be the beginning of social services in Peru. She spent the last three years of her life in the home of Don Gonzalo de Massa, a government official. Rose died there on August 24, 1617, and is the patroness of Peru and South America. She is also the first canonized saint of the Americas.

Carlo Dolci. *St. Rose of Lima,* (1616-86)
Palazzo Pitti, Florence, Italy

St. Louis was born in Poissy, France, on April 25, 1214. He was the son of King Louis VIII and Blanche, daughter of Alfonso of Castile and Eleanor of England. King Louis VIII died when Louis was twelve years old, and his mother became regent for him. At the age of nineteen, he married Margaret, the eldest daughter of Raymund Berenger, Count of Provence. They had eleven children, five sons and six daughters. In 1235, Louis came of age and took over the government of France. Devoted to God and his people, he was a model ruler who promoted peace and justice in his kingdom. He cared for the poor, founded hospitals, promoted learning, and lived humbly and prayerfully among his people. The system of justice he established settled disputes among his subjects by just procedures rather than violence or fraud.

Louis defeated King Henry II of England at Taillebourg in 1242 and made a treaty with him in 1259. At the same time, his devotion to Christ inspired him to lead a Crusade to the East in 1248. Louis captured Damietta in Egypt, but in 1250 was captured and taken prisoner by the Saracens. He was eventually released and with his army sailed to Palestine, where he remained until 1254. He returned to France in 1254 upon hearing of the death of his mother, who had been acting as regent during his absence.

Louis announced another Crusade in 1267 and left for the East in 1270. During the voyage, he became ill with typhus and died at Tunis, on August 25, 1270. Though his two Crusades into the Holy Land largely failed, his heroic example and loyalty to his army left a lasting memory for his successors and his people. He is one of the patrons of France.

El (Domenico Theotocopuli) Greco. *St. Louis (1215-70) and his Page*, Louvre, Paris, France

St. Monica, the mother of St. Augustine, was born in Tagaste, North Africa, about 332. Married to a pagan, Patricius, she had three children, two sons and a daughter. Because she recognized his extraordinary gifts, she tried to give Augustine the best education possible. Above all, she wanted him to use his gifts for God and the Catholic faith. Through her efforts, Patricius was converted to Christianity in 370. He died one year later.

Augustine disappointed her by choosing a life of pleasure, accepting the Manichaean heresy, and rejecting Christianity. Turning to God, Monica spent herself in earnest prayer for her wayward son. A priest whose advice she sought said to her, "It is not possible that the son of so many tears should perish."

Monica followed her son to Rome in 383 and then to Milan in 386. There she learned he was converted to Christianity. She joined him in preparing for his baptism by St. Ambrose on Easter, 387. As they were returning to Africa, Monica fell mortally ill at the seaport of Ostia. Augustine tells of her moving words of farewell before she died. "Son, nothing in this world now makes me happy. All my hopes have been fulfilled. All I wished to live for was that I might see you a Catholic and a child of heaven. God has given me more; I see you ready to give up everything and become his servant." She died in 387.

ST. AUGUSTINE   August 28
(354-430) bishop and doctor

One of the great Christian teachers of all time, St. Augustine was born at Tagaste, North Africa, on November 13, 354. His father, Patricius, was a pagan and his mother was St. Monica. Patricius was converted to Christianity in 370 and died one year later.

Augustine went to Carthage in 370 to study rhetoric and philosophy. While there, he met a woman with whom he would have a relationship until 385. She bore him a son, Adeodatus. He was deeply attracted to Manichaeism, but became disillusioned after meeting Faustus, the leading Manichaean teacher of that time. He left for Rome in 383 and opened a school of rhetoric. Disturbed with his surroundings, he went to Milan in 384 and accepted a post as master of rhetoric.

August thirsted for wisdom. He found what he was seeking as he listened to the preachings of St. Ambrose in Milan. Augustine describes his spiritual journey in his Confessions, which recall his great struggle with evil and sin and his final experience of God's guiding grace. "Late have I loved you, O Beauty ever ancient, O Beauty ever new!" Augustine's later life echoes with grateful praise for the God he discovered to be so good.

Monica followed him to Milan in 386 and was present at his baptism by St. Ambrose on Easter in 387. After his baptism, August deepened his own understanding of Christianity in the company of some friends. With Monica and several others, he went to Ostia in 387. Monica died there in November of 387 and Augustine returned to Rome.

In 388, Augustine returned to Tagaste, where he remained for three years. He was ordained in 391 as an assistant to Bishop Valerius of Hippo. He established a monastery in Hippo and staunchly defended the faith against Manichaeism and Donatism. He was consecrated bishop as coadjutor to Valerius in 395 and succeeded him in 396.

Augustine remained in Hippo for thirty-five years, preaching and writing. His most famous works are Of the City of God and Confessions. He engaged in controversy, received innumerable visitors seeking his counsel and traveled to distant cities as a spokesman for the Christian faith. Not only the people of his time, but later generations as well, would find him a brilliant teacher of the Gospel proclaimed by Jesus Christ. He died at Hippo on August 28, 430 and is a Doctor of the Church.

Mateo Cerezo. *St. Augustine*, (1626-1666)
Prado, Madrid, Spain

French School. *St. Gregory,* (17th century)
Private Collection, Agnew's, London, UK

SEPTEMBER

ST. GREGORY THE GREAT   September 3
(540-604) pope and doctor

St. Gregory was born in Rome in 540. His family was one of the few patrician families left in Rome after the ravages of the preceding century, and his father, Gorgian, was a wealthy man who owned property in Rome and Sicily. He was educated in Rome and became a public official. In 570, at the age of thirty, Gregory became the prefect of Rome. Though he was an honest and successful public servant and one of the richest men in Rome, he gave up his position of prominence to devote his life to God.

In 575, he converted his home into a monastery under the patronage of St. Andrew and the guidance of the monk, Valentius. He became a monk himself and established six more monasteries in Sicily. He was ordained by Pope Pelagius II and appointed papal ambassador to Constantinople in 579. In 586, he returned to Rome and became abbot of St. Andrew's monastery. After Pope Pelagius died of the plague in 590, Gregory was elected to the papacy, the first monk to be so honored.

Rome and the rest of Italy were being devastated by drought, famine, plague, and the fierce Lombard invaders. "What happiness is there left in the world?" Gregory asked in a sermon. "Everywhere we hear groans; our cities are destroyed, our land is a desert. See how Rome, the mistress of the world, has fallen." In 593, he negotiated a treaty with the Lombard king, Agiluf. Through negotiations and alliances with the Lombards, Franks, and Visogoths, he strengthened the Church's position in Italy, France, and Spain. At the same time, he continued to spread the Gospel to the ends of the earth, sending missionaries to England and other parts of Europe.

Gregory conceived of his English mission, according to a story, one day when he saw some young English slaves in the marketplace. "Who are you?" he asked. "We are called Angels," they replied. "Angels of God," the pope answered. In 596, Gregory sent forty monks headed by St. Augustine to bring Christianity to England.

Through the fourteen tumultuous years of his papacy, Gregory suffered from a chronic illness that left him bedridden for long periods of time. Yet, he continued his tireless service to the Church, and in his preaching and writing urged the people of his day to a courageous patience in their trials. He called himself "the servant of the servants of God," a title every pope since has adopted. He died in Rome on March 2, 604. He is one of the four great Latin Doctors of the Church, along with Sts. Augustine, Ambrose, and Jerome.

(first century) apostle and evangelist

The call of St. Matthew, the tax collector, to be one of the twelve apostles of Jesus is described in the Gospel which bears his name. "Jesus saw a man named Matthew at his post where taxes were collected. He said to him, 'Follow me!' And Matthew got up and followed him."

It is hard to imagine a more unlikely person for Jesus to call as a companion than Matthew. Tax collectors, as agents of a hated Roman government and members of a profession known for unfairness and greed, were despised by the Jewish people. They were excluded from the synagogue and the temple. No good Jew would have anything to do with them.

When Jesus invited Matthew to follow him and then ate at his house where Matthew's friends, outsiders like himself, were gathered, he heard the outraged comments of Capernaum's local leaders. "Why does he eat with tax collectors and sinners?" Jesus answered simply, "Those who are well have no need of a doctor; sick people do."

By calling Matthew, Jesus invited an outcast to enjoy the healing friendship of God. In a lesson of love, he showed that God wants all, no matter who they are, to share his life.

According to tradition, Matthew wrote down

Michelangelo Merisi da Caravaggio. *St. Matthew and the Angel,*
(1571-1610) San Luigi dei Francesi, Rome, Italy

the stories and words of Jesus in Aramaic, the ancient language of Palestine. The first Gospel had its origins in him. Among the evangelists he is symbolized by the figure of a man, because Matthew's Gospel begins with human origins of Jesus. There are reports that Matthew left Judea and preached in the East, where he was martyred in Ethiopia.

Francois Simon. *St. Vincent de Paul (1581-1660),*
Mission des Lazaristes, Paris, France

ST. VINCENT DE PAUL
(1581-1660) priest

St. Vincent was born in Pouy, France, on April 24, 1581. His family were French peasants and lived on a farm in Pouy. His father, Jean, recognizing his son's talents, resolved to give him a good education. Vincent attended the College of Dax and was educated by the Franciscan Recollects. He entered the University of Toulouse in 1596 to study theology and philosophy and was ordained there in 1600. Ambitious for a good comfortable position, he became one of the chaplains for Queen Margaret of Valois and tutored the children of the Count of Gondi.

Vincent came under the influence of Father Peter de Bérulle and his life changed. In 1617, while in the country, he heard the confession of a poor peasant and suddenly realized how badly the poor of France were being cared for. Resolving to give his life to serving the poor, he left the home of the Count and Countess of Gondi and began to work among prisoners and galley slaves, who suffered from deplorable conditions. He was officially appointed chaplain of the galley slaves in 1619.

He gathered companions, and in 1625, founded the Congregation of the Mission, or the Vincentians, as they are commonly known, to preach the Gospel to the poor and work for the education of the clergy. With St. Louise de Marillac, he established the Sisters of Charity in 1633 to care for the sick, the orphaned, and the aged. Through his inspiration, many of the wealthy and more fortunate were drawn to works of charity. The Society of St. Vincent de Paul, founded in 1833 by Frederic Ozanam in Paris, is dedicated to the service of the poor in parishes and dioceses throughout the world. Vincent died in Paris on September 27, 1660, and was named patron of all Catholic charitable societies by Pope Leo XIII.

STS. MICHAEL, GABRIEL, and RAPHAEL archangels

September 29

Holy Scripture speaks of angels as ministers of God in human affairs. St. Michael defends the honor of God against Satan. St. Gabriel announced to Mary the coming of Jesus. St. Raphael guided Tobias on his journey and brought healing to Tobit, his blind father.

As servants of God, the angels are instruments of God's hidden providence. They preserve us from harm, give God's wisdom and strength to humanity, and accompany us on our journey through life.

Raphael (Raffaello Sanzio of Urbino). *St. Michael Overwhelming the Demon*, (1483-1520)   Louvre, Paris, France

Juan Martin Cabezalero. *The Vision of St. Jerome,* (1633-73)
Christie's Images, London, UK

ST. JEROME

(340-420) priest and doctor

St. Jerome was born in 340 in Stridon, a small town in North Italy near today's Italian-Yugoslavian border. He was given an excellent classical education by his parents and was tutored by Donatus, the famous pagan grammarian, in Rome. As a result, Jerome became an expert in the Greek and Latin languages. In 360, at the age of eighteen he was baptized in Rome by Pope Liberius. After his baptism, he traveled throughout the Roman Empire and was acquainted with many of the leading Christians of his day. He settled at Aquileia in 370 and became acquainted with St. Valerian.

Jerome went to Antioch in 374. In a dream, he saw himself in judgment before Christ, who rebuked him for his vain pursuit of worldly wisdom. Touched deeply by the dream, Jerome withdrew into the wilderness where, beset by temptations of many kinds, he "threw himself at the feet of Jesus, watering his feet with tears of prayers and penance," as he said later. To occupy himself, he began an intense study of Hebrew under a Jewish teacher. He found this study extremely difficult, but it prepared him for one of his great life works. He was ordained by St. Paulinus and went to Constantinople about 380 to study Scripture under St. Gregory Nazianzen. When Gregory left Constantinople, Jerome went to Rome in 382.

Pope Damasus asked him to be his secretary and in this capacity Jerome began his monumental translation of the Bible from Greek into Latin; it is called the Vulgate. "Not to know the Scriptures is not to know Christ," Jerome said. At the same time, his learned commentaries on the Scriptures and his conferences and letters won him a devoted following, especially among the Christian women of Rome.

Jerome, however, had his share of critics who resented his biting tongue and caustic comments on Roman society. Stung by their attacks on him, in 385 he left Rome for the Holy Land, where he established a number of communities near Bethlehem. There he not only continued his study of Scripture, but heatedly engaged in the controversies raging on the Church of his day. Jerome was sometimes ill tempered and harsh in his dealings with others, yet he sought God's mercy again and again for himself and those he had injured.

When Alaric and his barbarians attacked Rome in 410, great numbers of Roman Christians fled to Palestine for safety. Jerome tried to arrange shelter for them and wrote, "I have put aside all my study to help them. Now we must translate the words of Scripture into deeds, and instead of speaking holy words we must do them." He died at Bethlehem of a long illness on September 30, 420. He is buried at St. Mary Major in Rome. St. Jerome is a Doctor of the Church.

ST. FRANCIS OF ASSISI
(1182-1226)

October 4

St. Francis was born at Assisi, Italy, in 1182. The son of a wealthy cloth merchant, he enjoyed the benefits of his father's success: good food, fine clothing, and entertainment, a busy social life, and a place in his father's business. Love of adventure prompted him to become involved in the wars then waged through the cities and regions of Italy.

On his way to battle at Spoleto one day, when he was in his early twenties, he became ill and heard a voice telling him to "serve the master rather than men." Returning to Assisi, he experienced a great change within himself. Meeting a leper on the road, he embraced him and gave him alms. He began to visit the sick and support the poor. Praying one day before the crucifix in the deserted country church of St. Damian, he heard a voice saying to him, "Francis, go and rebuild my house; it is falling down." In 1206, the young man left and sold his goods to repair the poor churches in his neighborhood and to care for the needy.

His father, thinking his son had gone mad, summoned him before the bishops. Francis stripped off his clothes and giving them to his father said, "I have called you my father on earth,

Carlo Dolci. *St. Francis Receiving the Stigmata,* (1616-86)
Phillips, The International Fine Art Auctioneers, UK

but now I say, 'Our Father, who art in heaven.'" He left his father's home to follow Christ as a poor man, vowing to keep the words of the Gospel literally. Francis wished to preach the kingdom of heaven, to give freely what he received, to possess neither gold nor silver.

Joyful, simple, a lover of people and nature, Francis soon attracted companions who shared his love of Christ and the Gospel. In 1210, he went to Rome to seek approval of his way of life from Pope Innocent III. Blessing his endeavor and officially recognizing the Franciscans, the pope afterwards told of a dream in which he saw Francis holding up the pillars of the Church. He was joined by St. Clare in 1212 and convened over five thousand Franciscans at Assisi in 1219 for the General Chapter of Mats.

With his call to return to the spirit of the Gospel, Francis gave new life to the Christian people of Italy and Europe. Missionaries were sent to Tunis and Morocco for the first time in 1219. He also traveled to the Holy Land where he preached to the Moslems and visited the places where Jesus lived and died. During this journey, he unsuccessfully tried to convert Sultan Malek al-Kamil of Egypt. His deep affection for the events of Jesus' life inspired him to recreate the Holy Child's birth at Christmas by erecting a creche at Grecchia in 1223. He loved the Passion of Jesus so much that he received the wounds of Christ known as the stigmata on his own body on the feast of the Holy Cross in 1224. "Nothing comforts me so much as to think of the life and Passion of our Lord," he said. "Were I to live till the end of the world I would need no other book."

In poor health and half blind, Francis died welcoming his Sister Death, while the Passion of Jesus was read aloud from the Gospel on October 3, 1226.

Claudio Coello. *Communion of St. Theresa of Avila*, (c. 1670)
Museo Lazaro Galdiano, Madrid, Spain

ST. TERESA OF AVILA
(1515-1582) abbess and doctor

St. Teresa was born at Avila, Spain, on March 28, 1515, the daughter of an influential family in that town. Lively and affectionate by nature, she made friends easily and adapted readily to any circumstance.

As a child she was drawn to religion. She and her small brother avidly read the lives of the saints and once even attempted to leave home to die for their faith among the Moors in Africa. They were quickly returned home.

Teresa's religious values weakened in her teenage years. In 1531, however, she suddenly decided to enter the Carmelite monastery at Avila over her father's objection. She was professed in 1538. After a period of sickness and religious mediocrity, she began to experience great graces of prayer in her late thirties. She described her experiences with remarkable skill in writings that have become spiritual classics. Her Autobiography, The Way of Perfection, and The Interior Castle have inspired and guided countless people in their spiritual lives.

Teresa decided to reform her own Carmelite community with the help of Sts. Peter of Alcantara and John of the Cross and she established new monasteries throughout Spain. Despite much opposition she went about her task with a good disposition and great common sense. She was both a mystic and a practical apostle.

As she lay dying, the Holy Eucharist was brought to her bedside. "O my Lord, now it is time that we may see each other," she exclaimed. She died at Alba de Tormes, Spain, on October 4, 1582, surrounded by her sisters who had been enriched so much by her wisdom and example. She is a Doctor of the Church.

(first century) evangelist

Born of a pagan family, St. Luke became a convert to the Christian faith. He accompanied St. Paul on his second missionary journey and was with the apostle during his final imprisonment in Rome. Paul calls him "my dear friend Luke" in one of his epistles.

Luke compiled the third Gospel. He describes at length the infancy of Jesus and emphasized the Lord's prayerfulness and his mercy. The great parable of the Prodigal Son is found in Luke. The evangelist writes sensitively of Jesus' regard for women as well as his interest in the underprivileged and the outcasts of his society.

In the Acts of the Apostles Luke relates the beginnings of the infant Church as it develops under the inspiration of the Holy Spirit.

He saw clearly the continuity of the Church from the time of Jesus to its later expansion into the Gentile world. In his writings the Church's roots go back to the traditions of Israel and its future will touch all the nations of the earth. The Holy Spirit, descending at Pentecost, guides her with surprising wisdom and power, leading individuals and the Church herself to undertake new ventures despite human reluctance and fear.

One tradition says that Luke died at Boeotia,

in Greece, at the age of eighty-four. He is patron of painters and physicians. In art he is represented by an ox because he begins his Gospel with the account of the priest Zachary sacrificing in the temple.

Johann Ulrich Loth. *St. Luke,* (c.1590-1662)
Wilanow Palace, Warsaw, Poland

Georges de la Tour. *St. Jude Thaddeus,* (1593-1652)
Musee Toulouse-Lautrec, Albi, France

    and
ST. JUDE
    (first century) apostles

Little is known of Sts. Simon and Jude except that they were chosen by Jesus as apostles and appear well down on the list of twelve. They do not figure prominently in the Gospel stories, as do some other apostles. After Jesus' Ascension there is no reliable account of what happened to them. Stories of their founding the Church in Syria and Egypt are groundless.

Unlike Sts. Peter and Paul, whose words and deeds are widely reported in Scripture and whose achievements dramatically affected the society of their day, Simon and Jude appear to have done little in their lives that was notable. Yet the Church celebrates them among her founders, seeing their preaching revealing God to us and their prayers aiding her growth.

The apostles were not all of one mold. Some, like Peter and Paul, were active public figures immersed in the controversy and changing movements of their time. Others, perhaps like Simon and Jude, may have taken a quieter path. Yet their voices too have been heard through all the earth.

Not only brilliant, active, and achieving

apostles communicate the faith. Some, also apostles, may pass on this treasure in simpler, unnoticed ways; ordinary sowers, they cast the seed of faith undramatically on a world waiting for harvest.

ST. CHARLES BORROMEO
(1538-1584) bishop

November 4

St. Charles, the son of Count Gilbert Borromeo and Margaret Medici, sister of Pope Pius IV, was born into a noble and aristocratic family in the castle of Arona on Lake Maggiore, Italy, on October 2, 1538. He was educated at the Benedictine abbey of Sts. Gratinian and Felinus at Arona. He studied Latin at Milan and then attended the University of Pavia. He received his doctorate in 1559. In 1560, at the age of twenty-three, his uncle, Pope Pius IV, appointed him Secretary of State and Cardinal Deacon of Milan, entrusting him with many responsible positions in the service of the Church. Largely through Charles' efforts, the Council of Trent finished its work of Church reform in 1562.

Ordained a priest in 1563 and appointed Bishop of Milan shortly afterwards, Charles began a lifelong labor to reform the ancient Christian city where he had been appointed bishop. Like his predecessor, St. Ambrose, he fostered the education of clergy, established the Confraternity of Christian Doctrine for the religious education of children, and cared for the poor. He himself lived a simple, sparing life, without concern for his own comfort.

Orazio Borgianni. *St. Carlo Borromeo,* (1578-1616)
Hermitage, St. Petersburg, Russia

Though he suffered from a speech defect, he constantly preached to his people who received his words as if from a messenger of God.

When plague struck the area of Milan in 1576, Charles mobilized all the resources at his disposal to minister to the sick and the dying. He cared for the plague-stricken with his own hands and comforted them in their anguish until the plague subsided in 1578.

Other parts of the Church received his attention as well. The English college at Douai, France, which prepared priests for that troubled country, was founded through his efforts. He visited the neighboring country of Switzerland in 1583 to support the Catholic faith there.

During his ministry as bishop, Charles had enemies among the civil administration and his own clergy. In 1569, while he knelt at prayer in church, an assassin, Jerome Donati Farina, a Humiliati priest, tried to murder him, but the bullet fell harmlessly from the cloak on his back.

On the evening of November 4, 1584, at the age of 46, he died in Milan after making his annual retreat at Monte Varallo.

virgin and martyr

St. Cecilia, according to Roman legend, was a young patrician woman of Rome who was a Christian. She was filled with love for God to whom she vowed her life and virginity. Forced into marriage by her father, she sang to God on her wedding day, praying for help. Soon after, Valerian, her husband, and Tiburtius, his brother, were miraculously converted to Christianity by a vision and gave themselves to the care of the sick and the burial of the dead.

They were martyred at Pagus Triopus, outside of Rome, along with a Roman official, Maximus, because they refused to sacrifice to the gods. Cecilia buried their bodies, and was herself brought to trial for her beliefs. So persuasive was she that her accusers converted to Christianity. Finally, the prefect, Almachius, sentenced her to be suffocated in the heated bath of her home. Despite the intense heat she was unharmed, so a soldier was sent to behead her. She was struck on the neck three times and lingered for three days before dying. A tomb marking her grave is found in the cemetery of St. Callistus in Rome. St. Cecilia is the patron of musicians.

Carlo Dolci. *St. Cecilia,* (1616-86)
Hermitage, St. Petersburg, Russia

El (Domenico Theotocopuli) Greco. *St. Andrew,* (1541-1614)
Casa y Museo del Greco, Toledo, Spain

ST. ANDREW   November 30
    (first century) apostle

St. Andrew came from Bethsaida, a town in
Galilee on the Lake of Genesareth. He became a
disciple of St. John the Baptist, who sent him to see
Jesus. After visiting the Lord, Andrew called his
brother, Simon Peter, to come and meet the
Messiah. Later, as Jesus was walking along the Sea
of Galilee, he saw Peter and Andrew casting their
nets into the sea. Jesus said, "Follow me and I will
make you fishers of men."

Andrew accompanied Jesus throughout his
public ministry, and his name appears in the story
of the feeding of five thousand in the desert. After
the death of Christ, he labored as a missionary in
Scythia, Greece, and Turkey and established the
Church at Constantinople. He was crucified on an
X-shaped cross at Patras, Acaia. St. Andrew is the
patron saint of Russia and Scotland.

ST. FRANCIS XAVIER   December 3
(1506-1552) priest

One of the greatest missionaries of the Church, St. Francis Xavier was born near Pamplona, Spain, at the castle of Xavier, on April 7, 1506. He entered the University of Paris in 1524 and received his degree of licentiate from the College of St. Barbara in 1528. While at St. Barbara, Francis befriended St. Ignatius Loyola, the founder of the Jesuits. He was among the first companions of Ignatius and was present with six others who took their vows in 1534 at Montmartre. Francis, along with Ignatius and four Jesuit companions, was ordained at Venice in 1537. In 1540, Ignatius Loyola appointed him to accompany Father Simon Rodriguez as the first Jesuit missionaries to the East Indies, then a Portuguese colony.

Appointed apostolic nuncio to the East, Francis left for India in 1541. After a long voyage and much hardship, he arrived at Goa on May 6, 1542. For eleven years, Francis labored along the coast of India and in Japan.

During his travels he would visit Cape Comorin, Malacca, the Moluccas, near New Guinea, and Montai, near the Philippines.

In village after village he preached the Gospel,

Peter Paul Rubens. *St. Francis Xavier Blessing the Sick*, (1577-1640)
Kunsthistorisches Museum, Vienna, Austria

struggling to learn the native languages and living simply on the food available to him. Along the Indian coast he baptized and instructed great numbers of native Christians who had been ill-treated by the European colonists.

On August 15, 1549, Francis entered Japan. With the aid of some Japanese converts he had a translation made of Christian teaching. In halting Japanese he recited it to all who would listen. A small nucleus of Christians was converted, and these became the faithful foundation of the Church in Japan. Francis returned to India in 1551 and was appointed the first Jesuit provincial of the East and India.

Longing to bring the Gospel to China, a land forbidden to foreigners, Francis made his way to Sancian, a small island near Hong Kong, but before he could embark on his new venture, he took ill and died on December 3, 1552.

Francis found enormous joy in his missionary life. As he wrote in a letter, "Here in this vineyard we cry to God: Lord, give me not so much joy in this life."

St. Francis Xavier is the patron of foreign missions.

ST. NICHOLAS
(fourth century) bishop

St. Nicholas was born into a wealthy family at Patara, Asia Minor. He was imprisoned during the persecution of Diocletian, attended the Council of Nicaea, and died at Myra, where he was buried in the cathedral. Nicholas was chosen Bishop of Myra and devoted himself to helping the poor.

Tradition says that Nicholas devoted himself to works of charity. Hearing that an impoverished father had to sell his three daughters into prostitution because he had no money for their marriage dowry, Nicholas threw a small bag of gold into the poor man's window on three different evenings, and his daughters were able to marry. Finally, he was discovered as the bearer of these gifts.

At one time, he saved three innocent young men from execution by the powerful civil governor, Eustathius. At another time he came to the aid of seamen who called for his help during a storm off the coast of Lycia. Suddenly appearing on their ship, he manned the ropes and sails beside the weary sailors and brought the vessel to port. Another tale relates that during a famine in his country, Nicholas was able through his prayers to guide some passing ships filled with grain to come to relieve his starving people.

Italian School. *Portrait of St. Nicholas,* (18th century)
Oratorio di San Niccolo, Vernio, Tuscany, Italy

Needless to say, with stories like these to his credit, Nicholas became a popular saint after his death. Seamen throughout Europe and Asia, as well as his own people, adopted him as their patron. His relics were carried to Bari, Italy, in 1087, after the Moslem invasion of Asia Minor. Countless churches in England, France and Germany bear his name. In Germany he became associated with Christmas, and as a giver of gifts on that holy day he is known in America as the kind and generous "Santa Claus."

French School. *St. Ambrose*, (17th century)
Private Collection, Agnew's, London, UK

ST. AMBROSE

(340 – 397) bishop and doctor

St. Ambrose, the son of a high Roman official, was born at Trier, Germany in 340. After the death of his father, the family moved to Rome. Ambrose studied Greek, law, and rhetoric and came under the tutelage of Anicius Probus, the praetorian prefect of Italy, who appointed him as his assessor. His ability was recognized by Emperor Valentinian, who appointed him governor of Liguria and Aemilia, in 372.

Auxentius, the Arian Bishop of Milan, died in 374. A new bishop had to be elected, and the Milanese Christians were divided into quarreling factions. In order to bring peace to the election, Ambrose went to the church to address the people. While he was speaking, someone cried out, "Ambrose, bishop!" The people enthusiastically took up the cry. Ambrose was not even baptized at the time. Over his objections and at the insistence of Emperor Valentinian, Ambrose prepared for baptism and his consecration as bishop. He was baptized and consecrated Bishop of Milan on December 7, 374. He was about thirty-five years old.

Ambrose proved to be a great bishop and served his people unselfishly. No one came to see him without being graciously received. His sermons and his celebrations of the liturgy filled his people with inspiration. St. Augustine, converted and baptized by Ambrose in 387, tells of leaving the church moved within his heart by Ambrose's words and personality.

The city of Milan was then an important political center of the Roman Empire. Ambrose, always a loyal Roman, was also a strong defender of the rights of the Church against Arianism. He was often a mediator between rival political groups in the imperial court. When Emperor Valentinian began to meddle in the affairs of the Church, Ambrose proclaimed, "The Emperor is in the Church, not over it."

Ambrose was an advisor to Emperor Gratian and convinced him to forbid Arianism in the West, in 379. When Maximus killed Gratian in battle in 383, Ambrose was able to keep him out of Italy and confine himself to France, Spain, and England. Despite their agreement, Maximus made plans to invade Italy in 387. After the invasion, the Eastern Emperor, Theodosius, was persuaded to come to the aid of Italy. Theodosius defeated Maximus and executed him in Pannonia. Valentinian II returned to Italy and Theodosius became ruler of both the Eastern and Western empires. At the urging of Ambrose, Theodosius publicly opposed Arianism within the Empire. After the murder of Valentinian II in 393, Theodosius, again at the insistence of

Ambrose, abolished paganism in the Empire.

Though Theodosius respected Ambrose, there were problems between them. In 390, Theodosius, angered by the murder of Butheric, the governor, massacred thousands of people in Thessalonica. Ambrose condemned him and called him to do public penance before he would administer the sacraments to him. Theodosius acquiesced. He died in 393 in the arms of Ambrose.

Courageous and holy, a bishop who upheld God's truth and the good of his people and his nation, Ambrose died at Milan on Good Friday, April 4, 397. St. Ambrose is a Doctor of the Church.

(d. 304) virgin and martyr

According to legend, St. Lucy was a young woman born at Syracuse, Italy. One day she went to the shrine of St. Agatha in Catania with her mother, who suffered from uncontrolled bleeding. While praying at the shrine, Lucy's mother was cured. Lucy decided to give up her worldly goods to serve the poor, took a vow of virginity, and broke off her impending marriage to a young nobleman in order to give her life entirely to God.

Her suitor was incensed at her action and accused her before the Roman consul of being a Christian who would not honor the laws of the Empire.

Bravely confessing her faith, Lucy was sentenced to be tortured by fire and boiling oil. She was unmoved by the ordeal and showed no sign of weakness. "God has granted that I should bear these things in order to free the faithful from the fear of suffering," she said. Though a sword was thrust through her throat, the young girl lived till communion was brought to her for her final journey to heaven. She died during the persecution under Emperor Diocletian in 304.

Francesco del Cossa. *St. Lucy,* (1435/6-c.1477)
Kress Collection, Washington D.C., USA

ST. JOHN OF THE CROSS

December 14

(1542-1591) priest and doctor

St. John was born at Fontiveros, Old Castle, Spain, in 1542. He was sent to school at Medina del Campo, but soon was apprenticed to a weaver. In 1559, he went to work for the governor of the hospital of Medina. He attended the Jesuit college at Medina and showed great talent as a student in theology and philosophy. John entered the Carmelite Order in 1563 and was ordained to the priesthood in 1567.

John was at Medina to celebrate his first Mass when he met St. Teresa of Avila. She spoke to him of her plans to reform the Carmelite Order. Though he had considered leaving the Carmelites. John decided to follow the primitive Carmelite rule and to assist Teresa in her task of reform. In 1568, joined by four companions, John founded the Discalced Carmelites. He took the name John of the Cross and monasteries were established at Duruelo, Pastrana, Mancera, and Alcala.

John suffered many misunderstandings and jealousies from fellow religious, even to the point of being imprisoned for nine months at Toledo in 1577. He continued, however, to write and preach on spiritual matters and devoted much time to guiding others in the spiritual life. His great treatises on the progress of the soul on its journey to

God, such as Dark Night of the Soul, Spiritual Canticle, and Living Flame of Love, have influenced spiritual theology profoundly.

In Dark Night of the Soul, written while he was imprisoned for nine months at Toledo, John described the path to holiness as a demanding journey that must be made in the dark night of faith. He explains the working of God's grace in the soul and the difficulties that face the beginners in the spiritual life. Spiritual Canticle and Living Flame of Love treat the mystical union that develops between God and the soul as it progresses in love. His writings demonstrate John's remarkable knowledge of the spiritual life which he expresses in poetry as well as prose. He is recognizable as a Doctor of the Church for his ability to guide people to a more perfect life.

John died at La Peneula Monastery in Andalusia, Spain, on December 13, 1591, repeating the words of the psalmist as Jesus had done, "Into your hands, O Lord, I commend my spirit."

ST. STEPHEN

(d. 34) first martyr

From early in the fourth century, the deacon Stephen has been honored by the Catholic Church on December 26, the day after Christ's birth. He is the first martyr, dying for his faith in Jesus, born of Mary. The story of his persecution and death before the Sanhedrin is told vividly in the Acts of the Apostles.

"As a deacon appointed by the apostles after Pentecost, Stephen was a man filled with grace and power, who worked great wonders and signs among the people. Certain members of the so-called 'Synagogue of Roman Freedman' (that is, the Jews from Cyrene, Alexandria, Cicilia, and Asia) would undertake to engage Stephen in debate, but they proved no match for the wisdom and spirit with which he spoke.

"Those who listened to his words were stung to the heart; they ground their teeth in anger at him. Stephen meanwhile, filled with the Holy Spirit, looked to the sky above and saw the glory of God and Jesus standing at God's right hand. 'Look!' he exclaimed, 'I see an opening in the sky and the Son of Man standing at God's right hand.' The onlookers were shouting aloud, holding their hands over their ears as they did so. Then they rushed at him as one man, dragged him out of the

Francia, (Francesco di Marco Raibolini) Il. *Saint Stephen*, (1450-1517)
Galleria Borghese, Rome, Italy

city, and began to stone him. The witnesses meanwhile where piling their cloaks at the feet of a young man named Saul. As Stephen was being stoned he could be heard praying, 'Lord Jesus, receive my spirit.'"

"The love that brought Christ from heaven to earth raised Stephen from earth to heaven," says St. Fulgentius. Stephen's love gave him courage before an angry mob and prompted him to pray like Jesus for his persecutors.

St. Stephen, St. John the Apostle, and the Holy Innocents, whose feasts occur on the following days of December, are seen as special companions of Jesus. They are examples of the different ways of martyrdom for Christ. Stephen voluntarily accepted death and was executed for his faith. John willed to die for Christ, but was not martyred. The Holy Innocents died for Christ without understanding what was happening to them.

(d. 100) apostle and evangelist

St. John was born in Galilee, the son of Zebedee the fisherman. Along with his brother, St. James the Great, he was called by Jesus to be one of his closest disciples. He witnessed the Transfiguration on Mount Tabor and Jesus' agony in the Garden of Gethsemani. As the "disciple whom Jesus loved," John rested his head on the Lord's breast at the Last Supper and was the only one to stand with Mary beneath the cross on Calvary. Jesus committed John to his mother's care, "Woman, behold your son," and in turn gave Mary to him as his mother, "Son, behold your Mother."

On Easter Sunday, John ran with Peter to see the empty tomb and believed that Christ was risen from the dead. After Pentecost, at the temple gate with Peter, he healed a cripple who sat begging alms. John was a founder of the Church at Jerusalem and after some years went to Ephesus in Asia Minor. Here, according to tradition, he lived with Mary till her death and authored the great Gospel and Epistles that bear his name.

Early sources say that because of his teachings he was banished to the island of Patmos for a time and there wrote down revelations from heaven in a book called The Apocalypse or Revelation. He opposed heretics who denied that Jesus was God

Francisco Ribalta. *St. John the Evangelist,* (1565-1628)
Prado, Madrid, Spain

and taught his followers the great commandment of love. St. Jerome write that as an old man too weak to engage in any activity, he would repeat to those he met, "My little children, love one another." When someone asked him why he repeated these same words over and over, he replied, "Because it is the Lord's teaching, and if you keep it you do enough."

He died at Ephesus when he was about ninety-four years old.